Macropods

A Guide to Keeping Kangaroos & Wallabies

Including Potoroo, Bettongs, The Quokka,
Pademelons, Rock Wallabies & Wallaroos

by Donna Racheal

4th Edition, Jan 2023

Published by:
Paw Printz 'Caring for Companion Animals'
P.O Box 467, Monbulk, VIC 3793
Email: info@pawprintz.com.au

All photographs by Donna Racheal

Acknowledgements
A special thanks goes to those institutions that shared with me their wealth of knowledge. As well as friends and family who offered their support and understanding throughout the production of this book.

Disclaimer

For further information visit our website:
www.pawprintz.com.au

CONTENTS

Eastern Grey Kangaroo *Macropus giganteus*

In the Beginning .....

Australia's unique mammal fauna is to some extent explicable with the Australian continent itself. It was once part of Gondwanaland - a southern super-continent that also included those landmasses we now recognise as South America, Africa, India, Madagascar and New Zealand. Through continental drift they separated. In the course of some 40 million years during which Australia was adrift in the Indian Ocean, its native mammals underwent a considerable adaptive radiation.

The native mammals of Australia are derived from two sources - The oldest are descendants of *monotremes* and *marsupials* that were on the continent when it broke away from Antarctica 55 million years ago. The other, *placental mammals,* did not migrate to Australia until it had begun to collide with Asia (some 15 million years ago).

Monotremes
There are only two living species in this group of mammal in Australia – the Platypus and the short-beaked Echidna.

Marsupials
Australia has over 120 species of marsupials. They have taken up most of the available niches in Australia. However, there are no freshwater or sea dwelling marsupials, nor ones capable of true flight. Their young are born at an early stage of development and nurtured during a period of development and growth outside the mother's body attached to teats of abdominal mammary glands, which are often (but not always) enclosed in a pouch.

Marsupials can be split into two main groups:
Herbivorous – those that largely feed on plants (some are omnivorous)
Carnivorous – those that feed mainly on animals and insects.

Placental Mammals
Australia has relatively few placental mammals. Bats were able to fly in, while rats island-hopped by floating on rafts whenever washed out to sea in floods. There are approximately 50 species of native rats – many only mouse sized, and around 60 species of bats in Australia.

Wildlife in Captivity

Australia has one of the highest extinction rates of native mammals in the world – nearly 25% of all known species are extinct, endangered or vulnerable. Government funding is limited, public institutions often have their hands unwillingly tied behind their backs, and private keeping is frowned upon in many states and territories. So what's the answer?

Many people throughout Australia – with or without certified education – have an interest in, the knowledge of or are just plain passionate about Australian native wildlife. We can't all become Zoo-keepers or own private fauna parks, but we still care enough to be genuinely concerned at what's happening, and want to make a difference.

There are those of us that can financially donate towards the many worthwhile causes in circulation. And those of us that give up our valuable time to aid with hands-on help on many different projects. Then there's one step further – those of us who wish to keep native wildlife in captivity.
I have heard of various reports of 'tame' wild animals turning on their keepers. Even a 120g Sugar Glider can inflict a nasty bite – image what a 60kg male Grey Kangaroo could do? Wild animals belong in the wild. So why did I write this book?

For as long as many of us have made Australia home, many different species of native wildlife have been bred in captivity – for a multitude of purposes. Zoos with their education and endangered breeding programs, Universities with their research, and private fauna parks for public recreation. So what happens to the surplus stock? Or when the gene-pool become inter-bred? Or to a rescued animal that comes into keeping – but is unsuitable to be re-released, and yet (under law) is not allowed to be put on public show if it has any visual impairment? Euthanasia? Common sense says this is where private keepers come into being.

Under no circumstances is it permissible to take native fauna from the wild for the sole purpose of 'having a pet'.

Wild animals are not domesticated.

Red-necked Wallaby *Macropus rufogriseus*

Like most people – I once thought possums ate gum leaves and wallabies ate grass. And they do. But there's more. Like our domesticated cats and dogs – native wildlife require a varied and balanced diet. They require specific handling, adequate space, and environmental stimulation.

I do not wish to enter into the debate of 'wildlife as pets'. That was not the reason I became so determined to write this book. It was the animals' well being - each individuals welfare that prompted me into spending many months researching the information to help make those species lives whom are kept in captivity, happier and healthier.

Whether I agree with it or not – the fact remains that today many native species are kept in captivity for the purposes of private admiration. I just wanted to do my bit to ensure they get as much quality care each and every one of them deserves.

MACROPODS
A Kangaroo or a Wallaby?

Both belong to the family Macropodoidea (meaning large feet), and altho' they have many characteristics in common; they also have rather definite differences.

Description

Both Kangaroos and wallabies have powerful hind legs and long feet, with most moving via a hopping action. With the exception of the Musky-rat kangaroo, Macropods bound on their hind legs when needing to move fast – the larger kangaroos being able to travel up to 8 metres in a single bound! They cannot walk as such, and have great difficulty moving backwards. An interesting point – when swimming they move their legs one at a time rather than in unison.

The animals are less efficient when moving slowly, needing to use their tail as an ex- tra leg. But when travelling quickly the tail is utilised as a rudder, and to achieve perfect balance - allowing the kangaroo to use all four legs to attack during a fight.

It is believed the kangaroos which lived during the dinosaur period were arboreal, their tail was prehensile and used to grip branches (much like todays possums), a function which seems to have been lost in todays larger macropods.

Two noticeable differences between kangaroos and wallabies are that the wallaby's tail is thinner and more rat-like while is hind feet are shorter and more powerful because of the uneven ground it inhabits.

Females of the macropod family have a permanent upward-facing pouch where they suckle and protect their young. As well as providing safety for the Joey, it also allows for it to feed on grass when the mother is grazing.

Of the 60 plus species of macropods recorded, their appearances can vary greatly depending on the habitat of which they are found. Different sizes, coloured fur and special features have been adapted to survive within their chosen environment. Kangaroos can be up to 180cm tall (Red kangaroo) and as small as 15cm (Musky-rat kangaroo). Wallabies tend to be smaller than kangaroos and wallaroos, and have a cone-shaped face.

But whatever their size, both have an excellent sense of sight and smell. Their ears can rotate 180 degrees to help warn them of approaching danger from any direction.

Habitat

There seems to be a kangaroo or wallaby to fit every type of habitat found within Australia (with the exception of above the snow-line). The larger kangaroos are commonly found on the plains and in scrub country, whereas wallabies tend to inhabit rocky or treed areas. Eg: the Red kangaroo lives on the hot open plains, the rock wallaby easily travels across rocky hillsides, the rat-kangaroo can be found in open scrub and the potoroo runs through the tangled flora on the rainforest floor.

Diet

With the exception of Pademelons, Hare-wallabies and the Swamp Wallaby who feed on leaves, most kangaroos and wallabies are grazing animals – eating the green grass found close to the ground. They have two front teeth on the top jaw which the bottom front teeth do not meet. Rather than cutting the grass, the kangaroo pulls at the green leaves until it tears away. Some wallaby species prefer berries and fruit.

Another difference between them is in the use of their hands for feeding. Wallabies use their paws to hold and pick up fruit/berries, having a firm grip to pull food from the bushes, while kangaroos use their front legs for balancing when feeding.

Mostly a nocturnal animal, they will move around between rest periods during the day. Macropods need water, but are very vulnerable to attack whilst drinking. Being very careful when approaching water to check for predators, they will often wait until late afternoon or early morning before leaving the protection of trees and bushes.

Breeding

Kangaroos and wallabies can mate at any time of year. The Joey is born after 5 weeks (depending on habitat conditions); is hairless, with no eyes, and about the size of your thumb. It makes its own way into the pouch, attaching itself to its mother's teat – which then swells in its mouth to hold the Joey firmly in place. After 6-8 months it will leave the pouch for short periods, and is permanently out by 9 months of age.

One of the astonishing things about most Macropods is that the female can be continually pregnant from the time she reaches sexual maturity (around the 2 yr mark). Within days of giving birth, a second foetus appears, but will not grow until the first born Joey leaves the pouch (or dies). *This is known as embryonic diapause.* Thus, the female can have a small 2cm long Joey on one teat, an older Joey which has left the pouch, but returns for milk during the day from another teat, and a foetus waiting to develop within her body. Of her four teats, each one will give different types of milk depending on the need of each individual Joey. Amazing!

Black-tailed Wallaby *Wallabia bicolor*

Brush-tailed Rock Wallaby *Petrogale pencillata*

SMALL MACROPODS

Potoroo
Long-nosed Potoroo   *Potorous tridactylus*

Bettongs
Rufous Bettong   *Aepyprymnus rufescens*
Tasmanian Bettong   *Bettongia gaimardi*
Brush-tailed Bettong   *Bettongia pencillata*

Quokka   *Setonix brachyurus*

Pademelons
Tasmanian Pademelon   *Thylogale billardierii*
Red-legged Pademelon   *Thylogale stigmatica*
Red-necked Pademelon   *Thylogale thetis*

Rock Wallabies
Unadorned Rock Wallaby   *Petrogale inornata*
Brush-tailed Rock Wallaby   *Petrogale pencillata*
Yellow-footed Rock Wallaby   *Petrogale xanthopus*

LONG-NOSED POTOROO
Potorous tridactylus - Kerr 1792

Size: Head & Body 34-38 cm; Tail 22-24 cm
Weight: Males 1.2 kg; Females 1.0 kg

Potorous – Aboriginal name for the species in the region of Port Jackson.
tridactylus – 'three toed' refers to the three toes of the hindfoot.
Also known as **Long-nosed Rat-Kangaroo, Wallaby Rat.**

Description
The long-nosed Potoroos fur is a red-brown to grey colour above, and paler below. It has a tapered nose with a bare patch of skin just above the nostrils. The ears are short and round. The tip of its relatively short tail is white.

Habitat
Found in coastal and near-coastal areas in Victoria, New South Wales and Tasmania (including King & Flinders Islands') the long-nosed Potoroo is widespread in most forest types including cool rainforest, wet sclerophyll and heathland that provides thick ground cover.

Diet
Underground fungi form the main part of the long-nosed Potoroos diet, which it unearths at night with its strongly clawed forepaws. Roots, tubers and soil invertebrates are also eaten.

Social Interaction
Solitary and mainly nocturnal, this Potoroo can sometimes be spotted at dusk. It hops on its back legs when moving quickly along the network of runways formed through thick ground cover. During the day it sleeps in a roughly constructed nest of vegetation over a scrape in the ground, close to a shrub or tussock. Its prehensile tail is used to carry nesting material.

Breeding
The long-nosed Potoroo breeds throughout the year, peaking in late winter/ early spring, and again in summer. The female has a well-developed forward opening pouch, carrying only one young at a time. Gestation is 38

days. The young remains in the pouch for 4-4 ½ months, then stay close to its mother, continuing to suckle until around 5-6 months. Females become sexually mature at 12 months of age. Although known to live to 7 years in the wild, the average life expectancy is 4-5 years.

Status
Large regions of habitat along the eastern coast of Australia have been lost to this Potoroo due to land clearing.

SUGGESTED DIET
Per Animal - Per Day
Increase during breeding season

A mixture of VEGETABLES (pumpkin, silverbeet, lettuce, artichokes, parsley, endive, carrot tops, sweetcorn, mushrooms, sweet potato) & GREENS (green oats, tree lucerne) and a little FRUIT (apple, banana, etc)

Extras (every 2nd day)
Insects (mealworms, crickets), 1x Boiled Egg; 1 tbsp Macropod Mix

Optional (once a week)
1x Nuts (peanuts, almonds, etc), 1 tsp Sunflower seeds, Sprouted alfalfa

Ad Lib - **Meadow Hay**

CLEAN WATER AVAILABLE AT ALL TIMES

Recommended Enclosure Size

Minimum enclosure floor area	Maximum number of animals	Minimum Height (roofed encl.)	Increased floor area per additional animal
20 sq. m	1	2 m	10 sq. m

** Watch for signs of incompatibility as relationships can change quickly*

RUFOUS BETTONG

Aepyprymnus rufescens - Gray 1837

Size: Head & Body 37-39 cm; Tail 34-39 cm
Weight: Males 3 kg; Females 3.5 kg

Aepyprymnus – 'high-rump' referring to the height of the animals hips over the rest of its body when on all fours.
rufescens – 'reddish' referring to its reddish tinted fur.
Also known as **Rufous Rat-kangaroo.**

Description
Although closely related *Bettongia*, this genus is distinguished by the presence of hairs on the central part of its muzzle. The Rufous Bettongs' head is broad and its ears pointed.

Habitat
Extinct in Victoria, the Rufous Bettongs' range is limited to the eastern parts of Queensland and northern New South Wales. It inhabits well-grassed open eucalypt forest, or woodland.

Diet
The Rufous Bettongs principal food source is tubers and roots of a variety of native and introduced perennial herbs, which it digs up with its strongly clawed forepaws. Fungi, grasses, sedges and herbs also feature in its diet. It is commonly found feeding in open pasture adjacent to forested areas.

Social Interaction
A nocturnal and somewhat aggressive animal, by day the Rufous Bettong sleeps in a nest of vegetation constructed over a shallow scrape, usually found under a tussock or fallen log. Its uses its prehensile tail to carry the grasses used as nesting material for the number of nests within its territory.

Breeding
Breeding is continuous throughout the year for the Rufous Bettong. The female has four teats in a forward opening pouch. The gestation period is 22-24 days. A single young is born in the nest. It vacates the pouch at

around 4 months of age, and will follow its mother at heel whilst still sucking until around 6 months old. A female reaches sexual maturity at 11 months of age, and can produce up to 3 young per year.

Status
Although no longer present in Victoria and uncommon in New South Wales, the Rufous Bettong appears to be secure in Queensland.

SUGGESTED DIET
Per Animal - Per Day
Increase during breeding season

1 cup of SEASONAL FRUIT (Apple, Banana, Pear, etc)
2/3 cup of VEGETABLES (Corn, Carrot, Sweet Potato, Silverbeet)
2 tsp Mammal Meat Mix; 3 Dog Kibble

Extras (every 2nd day)
2 tsp Boiled Egg & Cheese; Greens, Sprouted Seed
Insects (Mealworms, Crickets, Etc)

Optional (once a week)
1x Sultanas, Sunflower seeds, Almonds
1 tsp Glider Nectar mix

Ad Lib - **Meadow Hay**

CLEAN WATER AVAILABLE AT ALL TIMES

Recommended Enclosure Size

Minimum enclosure floor area	Maximum number of animals	Minimum Height (roofed encl.)	Increased floor area per additional animal
20 sq. m	1	2 m	10 sq. m

** Bettong Males Should Not Be Housed Together*

TASMANIAN BETTONG
Bettongia gaimardi - Desmarest 1822

Size: Head & Body 31-33 cm; Tail 29-34 cm
Weight: 1.2 - 2.25 kg (av. 1.7 kg)

Bettongia – Aboriginal for 'small wallaby'
gaimardi – named after the french naturalist J.P. Gairmard.
Also known as **Eastern Bettong, Gaimard's Rat-kangaoo.**

Description
The Tasmanian Bettong has coarse brownish-grey coloured fur above, with greyish-white underneath. It has short round ears and a long prehensile tail, which usually has a white tip.

Habitat
Although widely spread across the eastern half of Tasmania, its distribution is patchy. It is the only Bettong now endemic to Tasmania, living in dry sclerophyll forests and woodland with an open grassy understorey. It is most abundant where soils are low in nutrients.

Diet
At night it digs for the fruiting bodies of the underground hypogeal fungi – the bulk of its diet. Other plant materials (leaves, seeds, mushrooms, roots, bulbs and gum from acacia shrubs) and some insects are also eaten.

Social Interaction
Being a solitary and territorial animal, the Bettong occupies a large home range (males 65ha, females 45ha). By day it sleeps in a nest built from woven dry grass and stringybark (carried in its tightly coiled tail) located in shallow depressions under fallen tree limbs or among tussocks in open grassy areas.

Breeding
Breeding occurs all year round. The gestation and oestrus cycle are similar in length 21-22 days. The female has four teats in a forwardly opening pouch. She rears one young at a time, which leaves the pouch at 3½

months, but continues to follow its mother until weaned at 6 months. Females become sexually mature at 12 months, and can produce two or three young in a year.

Status

This animal is wholly protected in Tasmania. Large areas of its habitat have been lost following clearfelling and the young regenerated forests are unsuitable for the Bettong. The few remaining high-density populations are on private land.

SUGGESTED DIET
Per Animal - Per Day
Increase during breeding season

1 cup of SEASONAL FRUIT (Apple, Banana, Pear, etc)
2/3 cup of VEGETABLES (Corn, Carrot, Sweet Potato, Silverbeet)
2 tsp Mammal Meat Mix; 3 Dog Kibble

Extras (every 2nd day)
2 tsp Boiled Egg & Cheese; Greens, Sprouted Seed
Insects (Mealworms, Crickets, Etc)

Optional (once a week)
1x Sultanas, Sunflower seeds, Almonds
1 tsp Glider Nectar mix

Ad Lib - ***Meadow Hay***

CLEAN WATER AVAILABLE AT ALL TIMES

Recommended Enclosure Size

Minimum enclosure floor area	Maximum number of animals	Minimum Height (roofed encl.)	Increased floor area per additional animal
20 sq. m	1	2 m	10 sq. m

** Bettong Males Should Not Be Housed Together*

BRUSH-TAILED BETTONG
Bettongia penicillata - Gray 1837

Size: Head & Body 30-38 cm; Tail 29-36 cm
Weight: 1.1 - 1.6 kg (av. 1.3 kg)

Bettongia – Aboriginal for 'small wallaby'
gaimardi – referring to the hairy tip on the animals tale.
Also known as **Woylie, Brush-tailed Rat-kangaroo.**

Description
This Bettongs fur is yellowish-grey above, lighter in colour on the chest and belly. It has a bare snout, short and broad head, plump body and long claws on the front paws for digging. Its long tail has a black brushy tip.

Habitat
Once common throughout the tussock grassland and woodlands of southern Australia, the Brush-tailed Bettong is now only found in small isolated colonies in Western Australia. Habitat with a clumped understorey of tussock grass and low woody scrub are important to its survival.

Diet
A nocturnal feeder, the Brush-tailed Bettong forage for underground fungi, bulbs, fleshy roots, seeds, insects and sap resin from hakea shrubs.

Social Interaction
The Brush-tailed Bettong spends its day resting in an elaborate dome-shaped nest made of grass or shredded bark, built over a shallow scrape in the ground, or under a bush or tussock. It carries the nesting material in its coiled prehensile tail. It is a solitary and aggressively territorial animal. When hopping, it holds its front paws against its chest.

Breeding
Breeding occurs throughout the year. A single joey is born after a gestation of 21 days. It suckles at one of 4 teats in the mothers forward opening pouch for 3 months. It then follows the mother at heel, sharing the nest until around 4 months of age (and the next joey leaves the pouch). Females

become sexually mature by 6 months of age (males 9-12 months), and under favourable conditions can produce one young every 3 months. Brush-tailed Bettongs are known to live 4-6 years.

Status

Rare and endangered – the main cause of this species decline is the predation by foxes and feral cats. Populations survive in locations where foxes have been contained.

SUGGESTED DIET
Per Animal - Per Day
Increase during breeding season

1 cup of SEASONAL FRUIT (Apple, Banana, Pear, etc)
2/3 cup of VEGETABLES (Corn, Carrot, Sweet Potato, Silverbeet)
2 tsp Mammal Meat Mix; 3 Dog Kibble

Extras (every 2nd day)
2 tsp Boiled Egg & Cheese; Greens, Sprouted Seed
Insects (Mealworms, Crickets, Etc)

Optional (once a week)
1x Sultanas, Sunflower seeds, Almonds
1 tsp Glider Nectar mix

Ad Lib - **Meadow Hay**

CLEAN WATER AVAILABLE AT ALL TIMES

Recommended Enclosure Size

Minimum enclosure floor area	Maximum number of animals	Minimum Height (roofed encl.)	Increased floor area per additional animal
20 sq. m	1	2 m	10 sq. m

** Bettong Males Should Not Be Housed Together*

QUOKKA
Setonix brachyurus - Quoy & Gaimard 1830

Size: Head & Body 46-49 cm; Tail 26-29 cm
Weight: Males 4 kg; Females 3 kg

Setonix – 'bristle claw' referring to the animals hairy hindfeet.
brachyurus – 'short-tailed' its tail which is only twice the length of its head.
Also known as **Short-tailed Wallaby/Pademelon.**

Description
The only member of this genus, the Quokka has a stocky body, a broad face, short rounded ears and a short tail. Its long, thick fur is a frizzled grey-brown with a tinge of rufous. The hairs on its feet cover the claws.

Habitat
Found in the southwest of Western Australia, including Rottnest and Bald Islands off Perth in heathland areas with a dense understorey. Fossil evidence suggests that the Quokka has always been restricted to this region.

Diet
The Quokka feeds on shrubs and fibrous grasses at night. During the summer months the plants they feed on become very low in nitrogen and water, resulting in many animals becoming anaemic with those farthest from fresh water often perishing.

Social Interaction
Forming groups of 25-150 individuals occupying a common territory, which very few animals leave. Adult males are dominant to females and juveniles, who themselves have no ranking. By day several individuals sleep together in shelters, which males will defend against intruders. On hot summer days the animals will fight for shelter close to the water. Quokkas have excellent thermo-regulatory ability at ambient temperatures up to 44ºc.

Breeding
On the mainland, the Quokka appears to be able to breed continuously, but on Rottnest Island the breeding season is limited from Jan-Mar. Sexual

maturity is reached at 8-13 months. The smaller female has four teats in a forward opening pouch. She rears a single young, which leaves the pouch at 5 ½ - 6 months. Independence is reached at around 8 months of age.

Status
One of the most studied marsupials in captivity, the Quokka is seen as common on Rottnest Island, although it is sparse in other areas.

SUGGESTED DIET
Per Animal – Per Day
Increase during breeding season

MACROPOD MIX Approx. 300 grams

Daily Extras
½ cup Chopped Carrot; Maize (small amount sprinkled on top of food)

Twice a week (small amount)
Sweet Potato, Apple, Greens

Ad Lib
Meadow Hay; Lucerne Hay (in winter)

Fresh branches when available (Eucalypt, Acacia, etc)

CLEAN WATER AVAILABLE AT ALL TIMES

Recommended Enclosure Size

Minimum enclosure floor area	Maximum number of animals	Minimum Height	Increased floor area for each additional animal
50 sq m	1	2 m	20 sq m

** Watch for signs of incompatibility as relationships can change quickly*

Long-nosed Potoroo *Potorous tridactylus*

Quokka *Setonix brachyurus*

Brush-tailed Rock Wallaby *Petrogale pencillata*

Tasmanian Pademelon *Thylogale billardierii*

TASMANIAN PADEMELON
Thylogale billardierii - Desmarest 1822

Size: Head & Body 56-63 cm; Tail 32-42 cm
Weight: Males 7kg; Females 4kg

Thylogale – 'pouched weasel' the latter half being inappropriately named.
billardierii – named after the botanist J.J.H. la Billardiere.
Also known as **Red-bellied Pademelon, Rufous Wallaby.**

Description
The Tasmanian Pademelons' fur is dark brown to dark grey-brown, with a reddish-brown to buff belly. Males are considerably larger than females, with muscular forearms and chest.

Habitat
Before the turn of the century this Pademelon was common in southern Victoria. Today it is the only species of Pademelon found in Tasmania, in areas where there is dense undergrowth, including lowland rainforest, wet forest, coast scrub, and wet gullies in dry forests.

Diet
A nocturnal animal, the Tasmanian Pademelon emerges at twilight to feed on soft grasses and herbs, as well as tree seedlings and taller shrubs.

Social Interaction
Although a solitary animal, several may come together to feed. The male is territorial, and will boldly attack any intruder. Home ranges are quite large (up to 170ha), with individuals traveling up to 2km in the search for food. It shelters during the day in amongst the cover provided by dense vegetation.

Breeding
Breeding is throughout the year - the majority of births occurring in autumn or early winter. Mating occurs within one day of the female giving birth – the new embryo remaining dormant until the pouch is vacated. The gestation period is 30 days. One young are born, and remain in the pouch

for 6-7 months, being weaned at 10 months. It then follows its mother until 14-15 months of age, at which time it has reached maturity.

Status

Although once found throughout Australia, the last recorded mainland Tasmanian Pademelon was on the eastern coastline in the 1930s. Predation by the Red Fox may have been the major factor in the species decline. Foxes do not occur in Tasmania, where the pademelons are found in abundance.

SUGGESTED DIET
Per Animal – Per Day
*Increase during breeding season

MACROPOD MIX
Adult male 400 grams; Adult female 400 grams; Juveniles 300 grams

Extras
½ cup chopped Carrots (daily); Apple, Sweet Potato (twice a week)
Maize (small amount sprinkled on food)

Optional
Peanuts, Mushrooms, Greens, Fresh Lucerne

Ad Lib - Meadow Hay
Fresh branches when available (Eucalypt, Acacia, etc)

CLEAN WATER AVAILABLE AT ALL TIMES

Recommended Enclosure Size

Minimum cage or enclosure floor area	Maximum number of animals	Minimum Height	Increased floor area for each additional animal
300 sq m	1	1.8 m	150 sq m

Pademelons Require Dense Cover

RED-LEGGED PADEMELON
Thylogale stigmatica - Gould 1860

Size: Head & Body 46-49 cm; Tail 35-44 cm
Weight: Males 5kg; Females 4kg

Thylogale – 'pouched weasel' the latter half being inappropriately named.
stigmatica – 'point, pricked mark' referring to the faint stripe on its neck
and hip, which appear to have been 'pricked out' rather than 'filled in'.
Also known as **Northern Red-legged Pademelon.**

Description
The Red-legged Pademelon is a thick-furred, compact-bodied animal. It has
relatively short hindfeet, and an evenly furred, tapering tail. Easily
recognised by the rufous tinge to its cheeks, forearms and the inner and
outer surfaces of its hindlimbs, the fur is soft and grey brown, with cream
below.

Habitat
Found along the coast of Eastern Australia, from Cape York, down to mid
New South Wales. Distribution within the Red-legged Pademelons' range is
discontinuous, especially in the north where it appears to be limited by the
availability of vegetation to provide adequate cover. Their preferred habitat
is rainforest, but they can also be found in wet sclerophyll forests, and
occasionally in dry vine scrubs.

Diet
Grazing and browsing in open areas, this Pademelon feeds mainly on fallen
leaves. The Moreton Bay Fig is a major source of food in the southern parts
of its range – fruit of the Burdekin Plum in its northern parts.

Social Interaction
Usually a solitary animal it is active from late afternoon until early morning,
by day it sleeps in dense foliage in wet forests. When resting, its tail is
swung between the extended hindlegs and as it falls asleep, its head droops
forward until it rests on its tail or on the ground beside it.

Breeding
The Red-legged Pademelons breeding season appears to be continuous. Sexual maturity is reached at 12-17 weeks. The smaller female has four teats in a forward opening pouch. She rears a single young, which leaves the pouch at around 6-7 months. Independence is reached at 9 months.

Status
Although its status is secure, the Red-legged Pademelons available habitat has been severely reduced by the extensive clearing of rainforest.

SUGGESTED DIET
Per Animal – Per Day
Increase during breeding season

MACROPOD MIX
Adult male 400 grams; Adult female 400 grams; Juveniles 300 grams

Extras
½ cup chopped Carrots (daily); Apple, Sweet Potato (twice a week)
Maize (small amount sprinkled on food)

Optional
Peanuts, Mushrooms, Greens, Fresh Lucerne

Ad Lib - Meadow Hay
Fresh branches when available (Eucalypt, Acacia, etc)

CLEAN WATER AVAILABLE AT ALL TIMES

Recommended Enclosure Size

Minimum cage or enclosure floor area	Maximum number of animals	Minimum Height	Increased floor area for each additional animal
300 sq m	1	1.8 m	150 sq m

** Pademelons Require Dense Cover*

RED-NECKED PADEMELON
Thylogale thetis - Lessen 1837

Size: Head & Body 42-52 cm; Tail 35-43 cm
Weight: Males 7 kg; Females 4 kg

Thylogale – 'pouched weasel' the latter half being inappropriately named.
thetis – after the French exploration ship which visited Australia in 1825.
Also known as **Pademelon Wallaby.**

Description
This small macropod has a rufous tinge to its brownish-grey fur on the neck
and shoulders, whitish underneath, its tail is held rod-like when hopping.

Habitat
The Red-necked Pademelon is found on the eastern coast of Australia, from
south Queensland to just below mid-coast New South Wales. It inhabits
temperate coastal forests, rainforests and eucalypt forests in close proximity
to grasslands and shrublands.

Diet
This Pademelon moves around the forest, grazing and browsing. The
forepaws are often used to hold food and to manipulate material protruding
from its mouth.

Social Interaction
The Red-necked Pademelon spends most of its day sleeping in a shallow
depression in the leaf litter. When moving slowly it travels on all four paws,
dragging its tail behind in an unsupportive manner. A very timid animal, it
rarely moves more than 100m from the forest edge. Its home range is
usually between 5-30ha. When alarmed, one or two loud thumps made with
the hindfeet of the animals can often be heard. Males can become
aggressive.

Breeding
The majority of breeding takes place in autumn and spring in the northern
populations and summer in the southern populations. The smaller female

has four teats in a forward opening pouch. She rears a single young, which leaves the pouch between 6-6½ months. Independence of the young is reached at 10 months. Sexual maturity is reached at 12-17 months in females, 20 months in males.

Status

Altho common, the Fox and the Dingo are the Red-necked Pademelons main predator, and possibly large birds of prey. Where land has been cleared for agriculture or forestry, populations have increased.

SUGGESTED DIET
Per Animal – Per Day
Increase during breeding season

MACROPOD MIX
Adult male 400 grams; Adult female 400 grams; Juveniles 300 grams

Extras
½ cup chopped Carrots (daily); Apple, Sweet Potato (twice a week)
Maize (small amount sprinkled on food)

Optional
Peanuts, Mushrooms, Greens, Fresh Lucerne

Ad Lib - Meadow Hay
Fresh branches when available (Eucalypt, Acacia, etc)

CLEAN WATER AVAILABLE AT ALL TIMES

Recommended Enclosure Size

Minimum cage or enclosure floor area	Maximum number of animals	Minimum Height	Increased floor area for each additional animal
300 sq m	1	1.8 m	150 sq m

** Pademelons Require Dense Cover*

UNADORNED ROCK WALLABY
Petrogale inornata - Gould 1842

Size: Head & Body 50-54cm; Tail length 50-55cm
Weight: Males 5 kg; Females 4kg

Petrogale – 'rock weasel' aptly referring to the rocky terrain the animal
inhabits, it in no way resembles a weasel. *inornata* – 'unadorned'.
Also known as **Plain Rock-wallaby.**

Description
Characterised by its lack of distinctive colouration, the Unadorned Rock-
wallaby's fur is generally a grey-brown in autumn as it moults, to a sandy
colour through the rest of the year. It sometimes has a pale cheek-stripe and
its tail darkens towards the tip, often with a short crest.

Habitat
Occurring in open sclerophyll forest with associated rocky areas along the
Great Dividing Range in Queensland from Home Hill southwards to the
north bank of the Fitzroy River at Rockhampton, the Unadorned Rock-
wallaby is also found on some of the Whitsunday Islands.

Diet
The Unadorned Rock-wallaby emerges in the evening to feed.

Social Interaction
Spending its day asleep in a rock crevice, the Unadorned Rock-wallaby

Breeding
Breeding is continuous throughout the year, as long as there is a good
supply of water. Females have four teats in a forward opening pouch.
Gestation is 30-32 days, and a sin- gle young in normally born. This will
stay in the pouch for 7 months, and then follow its mother at heal until at
least 12 months of age. It will be weaned by the time its 9 ½ months old.
Sexual maturity reached at 18 months in both sexes. Males can become
aggressive.

Status
Common throughout most of its range.

SUGGESTED DIET
Per Animal – Per Day
Increase during breeding season

(approx. 300-400 grams of Wallaby Mix)
Adult males 3/4 cup
Adult females 1/2 cup
Juveniles 1/2 cup

Daily Extras:
Carrot (1 1/2 x amount of pellets)
Maize (small amount sprinkled on top of food)

Twice a week:
Sweet Potato, Apples
Vitamin E powder (once a week sprinkled on food)
Greens, Fresh Lucerne

Ad Lib
Meadow Hay
Fresh branches when available (Eucalypt, Acacia, etc)

CLEAN WATER AVAILABLE AT ALL TIMES

Recommended Enclosure Size

Minimum cage or enclosure floor area	Maximum number of animals	Minimum Height	Increased floor area for each additional animal
200 sq m	1	3 m	100 sq m

Watch for signs of incompatibility as relationships can change quickly

BRUSH-TAILED ROCK WALLABY
Petrogale pencillata - Gray 1825

Size: Head & Body 53-56 cm; Tail length 56-61 cm
Weight: Males 8 kg; Females 6 kg

Petrogale – 'rock weasel' although aptly referring to the rocky terrain the animal inhabits, it in no way resembles a weasel. *pencillata* – 'brush' referring to the brushy tip on the animals tail.
Also known as **Tuft-tailed or Mountain Kangaroo.**

Description
An extremely agile animal, its fur is brown above, grey on the shoulders and more rufous on the rump, with a paler chest and belly. It has a white cheek-stripe and black dor- sal stripe running from its forehead to the back of the head. Its feet and paws are dark brown to black, and the long cylindrical tail is longer than the head and body.

Habitat
Inhabiting the ranges north of the Queenland/New South Wales border, following the Great Dividing Range down into northern Victoria. This wallaby favours north-facing rocky outcrops in wet and dry sclerophyll forests, open woodland and rainforest gullies.

Diet
This Rock Wallaby emerges at night to feed on a wide variety of foliage from grasses, forbs, orchids, ferns to fruits, flowers and seeds when available.

Social Interaction
Resting by day in rock crevices, the Brush-tailed Rock Wallabies enjoys basking in the early morning and evening sunshine.

Breeding
Breeding occurs throughout the year. The female has four teats in a forward opening pouch. A single young is reared. The young leaves the pouch by 7 months of age, thereafter following its mother at heel until fully weaned at 9 1/2 months. Adults reach sex- ual maturity at around 20 months of age.

Status

Found in southeastern Queensland and northern New South Wales, altho'
some populations within its range have declined dramatically. The remnant
populations found in Victoria and western New South Wales are listed as
endangered.

SUGGESTED DIET
Per Animal – Per Day
Increase during breeding season

(approx. 300-400 grams of Wallaby Mix)
Adult males 3/4 cup
Adult females 1/2 cup
Juveniles 1/2 cup

Daily Extras:
Carrot (1 1/2 x amount of pellets)
Maize (small amount sprinkled on top of food)

Twice a week:
Sweet Potato, Apples
Vitamin E powder (once a week sprinkled on food)
Greens, Fresh Lucerne

Ad Lib
Meadow Hay
Fresh branches when available (Eucalypt, Acacia, etc)

CLEAN WATER AVAILABLE AT ALL TIMES

Recommended Enclosure Size

Minimum cage or enclosure floor area	Maximum number of animals	Minimum Height	Increased floor area for each additional animal
200 sq m	1	3 m	100 sq m

** Watch for signs of incompatibility as relationships can change quickly*

YELLOW-FOOTED ROCK WALLABY
Petrogale xanthopus - Gray 1855

Size: Head & Body 48-65 cm; Tail length 57-70 cm
Weight: Males 7 kg; Females 6 kg

Petrogale – 'rock weasel' altho' aptly referring to the rocky terrain the animal inhabits, it in no way resembles a weasel. *xanthopus* – 'yellow footed' referring to the orange-yellow hair on the upper side of its feet. Also known as **Ring-tailed Rock-Wallaby**.

Description
An attractive animal with fawn-grey fur over most of its body and white underneath. It has a distinct white cheek-stripe, a rich brown stripe from its head to half way down the back and reddish-brown patches behind the front legs and pale hip stripes. The forearms and forefeet are yellow to bright orange. The tail has brown and white rings.

Habitat
Adapted to semi-arid conditions, this animal can be found in SA, NSW and Qld. It inhibits the higher slopes of mountain ranges, usually containing large boulders scattered amongst scrubby vegetation, including a source of permanent drinking water.

Diet
Emerging at night to feed on grasses and herbs, the Yellow-footed Rock-Wallabys diet extends to include the leaves and steams of shrubs as the country dries out over summer.

Social Interaction
The Yellow-footed Rock-Wallaby lives compatibly in gatherings of up to 100 individuals. In hot weather it shelters in caves and rock crevices. On cooler days it can be seen sitting in the sunny spots on top of rock piles. The animals camouflage and habit of remaining completely still helps to avoid predators.

Breeding

Breeding is continuous, although it may stop during severe drought. Gestation is 30 days. The female has four teats in a forward opening pouch. She rears one young, which leaves the pouch at 6 ½ months. Independence is reached at 9 ½ months.

Status

Although common in the Flinders Ranges, the Yellow-footed Rock-Wallaby is rare within its Qld Range. Their main threat being competition for food by introduced goats.

SUGGESTED DIET
Per Animal – Per Day
Increase during breeding season

(approx. 300-400 grams of Wallaby Mix)
Adult males 3/4 cup; Adult females 1/2 cup; Juveniles 1/2 cup

Daily Extras:
Carrot (1 1/2 x amount of pellets)
Maize (small amount sprinkled on top of food)

Twice a week:
Sweet Potato, Apples, Greens, Fresh Lucerne
Vitamin E powder (once a week sprinkled on food)

Ad Lib
Meadow Hay
Fresh branches when available (Eucalypt, Acacia, etc)

CLEAN WATER AVAILABLE AT ALL TIMES

Recommended Enclosure Size			
Minimum cage or enclosure floor area	Maximum number of animals	Minimum Height	Increased floor area for each additional animal
200 sq m	1	3 m	100 sq m

Watch for signs of incompatibility as relationships can change quickly

Western Grey Kangaroo *Macropus fuliginosus*

LARGER MACROPODS

Wallabies

Agile Wallaby	*Macropus agilis*
Black-striped Wallaby	*Macropus dorsalis*
Tammar Wallaby	*Macropus eugenii*
Parma Wallaby	*Macropus parma*
Whiptail Wallaby	*Macropus parryi*
Red-necked Wallaby	*Macropus rufogriseus*
Black-tailed Wallaby	*Wallabia bicolor*

Wallaroos

Antilopine Wallaroo	*Macropus antilopinus*
Common Wallaroo	*Macropus robustus*

Kangaroos

Western Grey Kangaroo	*Macropus fuliginosus*
Eastern Grey Kangaroo	*Macropus giganteus*
Red Kangaroo	*Macropus rufus*

AGILE WALLABY
Macropus agilis - Gould 1841

Size: Head & body 71-85 cm; Tail 59-72 cm
Weight: Males 19 kg; Females 11 kg

Macropus – 'large foot' referring to the extreme length of the hindfoot.
agilis – 'agile' although not notably more so than any other of similar size.
Also known as **Sandy Wallaby, Kimberley Wallaby, River Wallaby.**

Description
A slender animal, the Agile Wallaby has sandy upper-parts and is white underneath. It has a stripe between the eyes and ears, with black margins to the ear. It has a distinct white hip-stripe. Its tail is long, and only slightly tapers, with a black tip.

Habitat
Inhabiting open forests along rivers, creeks and the adjacent grasslands. This Wallaby is the most widespread of the macropods in tropical Australia. In the Northern Territory it is abundant from the coast, to the inland hills.

Diet
Emerging late in the day and early evening, the Agile Wallaby feeds on native grasses, shrubs, and sedges, also digging up to 30cm into the soil for the roots of ribbon grass.

Social Interaction
A gregarious animal by nature, the Agile Wallaby lives in groups of up to ten individuals, but will congregate in even larger mobs when feeding. A nervous animal, it can be seen doing a lot of foot-stomping when alarmed.

Breeding
Breeding is continuous throughout the year. The female reaches sexual maturity at 12 months of age. She has four teats in a forward opening pouch. Gestation is 30 days. A single young is reared, which leaves the pouch at around 7 months. The young will remain dependent until 10-12 months of age. Males become sexually mature at 14 months.

Status

Being rather abundant, the Agile Wallaby is often seen as a pest in certain areas because of its effect on crops and pastures. Poisoning campaigns have been carried out is Western Australia and the Northern Territory, and there is still a bounty on its head in the cane-growing districts of Queensland.

SUGGESTED DIET
Per Animal – Per Day
Increase during breeding season

MACROPOD MIX:

Adult male	500 grams
Adult female	400 grams
Juveniles	300 grams

Daily
2/3 cup Carrot, 1/3 cup Maize

Twice a week
½ Sweet Potato, Apple
Greens, Fresh Lucerne

Ad Lib
Meadow Hay
Fresh branches when available (Eucalypt, Acacia, etc)

CLEAN WATER AVAILABLE AT ALL TIMES

Recommended Enclosure Size

Minimum enclosure floor area	Maximum number of animals	Minimum Height	Increased floor area for each additional animal
300 sq m	1	1.8 m	150 sq m

** Watch for signs of incompatibility as relationships can change quickly*

BLACK-STRIPPED WALLABY
Macropus dorsalis - Gray 1837

Size: Head & Body 53-82 cm; Tail 59-77 cm
Weight: Males 16 kg; Females 6.5 kg

Macropus – 'large foot' referring to the extreme length of the hindfoot.
dorsalis – 'back' refers to the dark stripe along the middle of its back.
Also known as **Scrub Wallaby.**

Description
The Black-striped Wallaby has brown upperparts with a very obvious mid-dorsal stripe from its neck to rump. It has a white spot on the cheek, behind the eye and is pale underneath. It has a distinctive hopping gait – head held low, body curved with rump tucked under and arms stretch sideways.

Habitat
Widespread through the wettest parts of southern Queensland and northern New South Wales, on either side of the Great Dividing Range this Wallaby stays well hidden in forested country with a dense shrub layer.

Diet
The Black-stripped Wallaby seldom ventures far from vegetation, normally feeding from dusk to dawn on pasture offering some tree protection.

Social Interaction
The Black-striped Wallaby spends much of its time undercover. During the day its rests under the shelter of shrubs. At dusk it moves along well-formed pathways through vegetation to the open country to feed on grasses and herbs, but is never far from cover. A social animal, it can be found in groups of up to 20 individuals or more. If disturbed, they will all move off in the same direction, quickly forming a single file.

Breeding
The female has four teats in a forwardly opening pouch. Gestation is 33-35 days. She usually rears one young, which stays in the pouch until around 7 months. Weaning is completed at 10-12 months of age. Females do not

become sexually mature until their second year (around 14 months), and 20 months for males. In the wild they have been known to live for 10-15 years, with older males living a solitary existence.

Status

Although seen as abundant in Queensland (in some areas it is classed as a pest species), the Black-striped Wallaby is listed as Endangered in New South Wales.

SUGGESTED DIET
Per Animal – Per Day
Increase during breeding season

MACROPOD MIX:

Adult male	500 grams
Adult female	300 grams
Juveniles	300 grams

Daily
2/3 cup Carrot, 1/3 cup Maize

Twice a week
½ Sweet Potato, Apple, Greens, Fresh Lucerne

Ad Lib
Meadow Hay
Fresh branches when available (Eucalypt, Acacia, etc)

CLEAN WATER AVAILABLE AT ALL TIMES

Recommended Enclosure Size

Minimum enclosure floor area	Maximum number of animals	Minimum Height	Increased floor area for each additional animal
300 sq m	1	1.8 m	150 sq m

** Watch for signs of incompatibility as relationships can change quickly*

TAMMAR WALLABY
Macropus eugenii - Desmarest 1817

Size: Head & body 58-65 cm; Tail 37-42 cm
Weight: Males 7.5 kg; Females 5.5 kg

Macropus – 'large foot' referring to the extreme length of the hindfoot of this genus. *eugenii* – taken from L'lle Eugene (now St. Peters Island) in the Neyts Archipelgo, where the first specimen was caught.
Also known as **Dama Wallaby, Tammar Pademelon.**

Description
A relatively small wallaby, the Tammar has dark grizzled, grey-brown fur with pale grey-buff below and slightly rufous on the sides of its body and limbs. It has a white cheek-stripe with a dark stripe between the ears. Its tail is rather short, and the forelimbs are extended when hopping.

Habitat
The Tammar Wallaby was once distributed in at least a dozen different areas, including offshore islands and detached mainland populations in both Western and South Australia. It can be found inhabiting coastal scrub, heath, dry sclerophyll forest and thickets in mallee and woodland areas.

Diet
Adapted to aridity, it can survive for long periods without drinking. Some coastal populations drink salt water - which implies very efficient kidneys.

Social Interaction
This Wallaby rests during the day in dense vegetation. It begins to move at dusk, but does not leave the scrub until after dark, grazing in open areas to return by dawn. Females are gregarious by nature, males often aggressive.

Breeding
Breeding is from summer to early winter, with most young born January–June. The female has four teats in a forwardly opening pouch. Gestation is 28 days. She rears a single young in the pouch for 8-9 months.

Independence is reached at 12-14 months of age. Females become sexually mature at about 9-12 months, males at around 22-24 months.

Status

Populations have been reduced in both South Australia and Western Australia, and it is now presumed extinct on many of the islands it once populated. Introduced populations are thriving on islands off New Zealand.

SUGGESTED DIET
Per Animal – Per Day
Increase during breeding season

MACROPOD MIX:

Adult male	400 grams
Adult female	300 grams
Juveniles	300 grams

Daily
2/3 cup Carrot, 1/3 cup Maize

Twice a week
½ Sweet Potato, Apple, Greens, Fresh Lucerne

Ad Lib
Meadow Hay
Fresh branches when available (Eucalypt, Acacia, etc)

CLEAN WATER AVAILABLE AT ALL TIMES

Recommended Enclosure Size

Minimum enclosure floor area	Maximum number of animals	Minimum Height	Increased floor area for each additional animal
100 sq m	1	1.8 m	50 sq m

** Watch for signs of incompatibility as relationships can change quickly*

PARMA WALLABY
Macropus parma - Waterhouse 1845

Size: Head & Body 45-52 cm; Tail 40-54 cm
Weight: Males 4-6 kg; Females 3-5 kg

Macropus – 'large foot' referring to the extreme length of its hindfoot.
parma – 'pama' Aboriginal name from the Illawarra region of NSW.
Also known as **White-throated Wallaby / Pademelon.**

Description
One of the smallest of the Wallabies, the Parma Wallaby has greyish-bown back and shoulders and a white throat and chest. It has a dark stripe running along the spine to its mid-back. Its white cheek-stripe is just visible. Around 50% of animals have a white tip on their long tails.

Habitat
Thought to be extinct on the mainland during the 1900's, a population was discovered in the late 1960's near Gosford, New South Wales. Now located on the mid-to-north coast of New South Wales, its preferred habitat is wet sclerophyll forests, thick with scrubby understorey close to grassy patches.

Diet
The Parma Wallaby emerges at dusk to feed on grasses and herbs. Its fecal pellets are distinctive in appearance, being flattened and squarish in shape.

Social Interaction
Generally a solitary animal, small groups can occur during feeding. By day, the Parma Wallaby shelters in low vegetation. When hopping it holds its forelimbs tightly alongside the body, remaining is an almost horizontal position. At a medium pace, the tail curves upwards in a shallow U-shape.

Breeding
Breeding season peaks February-June. Males reach sexual maturity between 20-24 months, females at 12-18 months of age. She has four teats in a forward opening pouch, and normally rears one young. Gestation is 35 days. The young leave the pouch at 7-8 months, but are not weaned until

9-10 months old. During this time the female may give birth to a second young. Independence is reach at around 15 months of age.

Status
Although rare and scattered populations occur in Australia, on Kawau Island off the North Island of New Zealand, where it was introduced last century, populations are dense, with control measures being put in place.

SUGGESTED DIET
Per Animal – Per Day
Increase during breeding season

MACROPOD MIX:

Adult male	400 grams
Adult female	300 grams
Juveniles	300 grams

Daily
2/3 cup Carrot, 1/3 cup Maize

Twice a week
½ Sweet Potato, Apple, Greens, Fresh Lucerne

Ad Lib
Meadow Hay
Fresh branches when available (Eucalypt, Acacia, etc)

CLEAN WATER AVAILABLE AT ALL TIMES

Recommended Enclosure Size

Minimum enclosure floor area	Maximum number of animals	Minimum Height	Increased floor area for each additional animal
100 sq m	1	1.8 m	50 sq m

* *Watch for signs of incompatibility as relationships can change quickly*

WHIPTAIL WALLABY

Macropus parryi - Bennett 1834

Size: Head & Body 75-92 cm; Tail 78-94 cm
Weight: Males 16 kg; Females 11 kg

Macropus – 'large foot' referring to the extreme length of the hindfoot.
parryi - named after Captain Parry, explorer and Commissioner of the Australian Agricultural company, who took a live specimen to England.
Also known as **Pretty-faced Wallaby, Grey-faced Wallaby.**

Description

A medium-sized kangaroo, the Whiptail Wallaby has a slender, dark-tipped tail that is a little longer than its head and body. It has a prominent white cheek-stripe, light brown should-stripe, and white hip-stripe. Its fur is a brownish-grey in summer, changing to a light grey in winter.

Habitat

Inhabiting undulating hilly areas in both wet/dry open sclerophyll forests with grassy understorey in southern Queensland and northern New South Wales.

Diet

This Wallaby can be found grazing in open country, particularly in the early morning and evenings on grasses, herbs and some ferns. It appears to get most of its water from dew and vegetation, as it is rarely seen drinking.

Social Interaction

It is a social species, often moving in groups of up to 50 individuals, comprising of subgroups of ten or less including adults and sub-adults of both sexes. When alarmed, the Whiptail Wallaby will run in a zig-zag manner. In the heat of the day it can be found resting in patches of shade.

Breeding

Breeding is continuous. When a female is in oestrous, a line of males will usually follow her, with the dominant one the closest. She has four teats in a forwardly opening pouch, usually rearing only one young. Gestation is

34-38 days. The young leave the pouch by 9 months, but remain dependent until around 10-15 months. Females do not breed until 18-24 months of age, and males do not normally have the opportunity until 2-3 years of age.

Status

Total clearing of forest has had a detrimental effect on the Whiptail Wallaby, but it appears to be widespread with big enough populations present in national parks and reserves to be viewed as common.

SUGGESTED DIET
Per Animal – Per Day
Increase during breeding season

MACROPOD MIX:

Adult male	500 grams
Adult female	400 grams
Juveniles	300 grams

Daily
2/3 cup Carrot, 1/3 cup Maize

Twice a week
½ Sweet Potato, Apple, Greens, Fresh Lucerne

Ad Lib
Meadow Hay
Fresh branches when available (Eucalypt, Acacia, etc)

CLEAN WATER AVAILABLE AT ALL TIMES

Recommended Enclosure Size

Minimum enclosure floor area	Maximum number of animals	Minimum Height	Increased floor area for each additional animal
300 sq m	1	1.8 m	150 sq m

Watch for signs of incompatibility as relationships can change quickly

RED-NECKED WALLABY
Macropus rufogriseus - Desmarest 1817

Size: Head & Body 71-82 cm; Tail 70-80 cm
Weight: Males 18-20 kg; Females 14 kg

Macropus – 'large foot' referring to the extreme length of its hindfoot.
rufogriseus - 'red-grey' refers to the reddish colour of its neck and
shoulders, and the grey colour of the rest of its body.
Also known as **Bennetts Wallaby, Eastern Brush-wallaby.**

Description
This large wallaby, has soft thick grey-fawn fur above with reddish-brown upper parts, especially over the neck and shoulder. The muzzle and paws are black. It has a dark brown stripe between the eyes and a white check stripe. The ears are black-edged and the tapering tail often had a dark tip.

Habitat
Distribution is patchy in the southern parts of eastern and western Victoria. Also occuring in southeastern South Australia, eastern New South Wales, southeastern Queensland, King and Flinders Islands and Tasmania. Red-Necked Wallabies inhabit wet and dry open forests and woodlands with a dense shrubby understorey, heathlands and sedgelands.

Diet
The Red-necked Wallaby feeds on grasses and herbs, both native and introduced such as lucerne.

Social Interaction
By day, this wallaby can be found sleeping in the dense scrub. Adults have a stable home range and are sociable by nature. Young female wallabies often settle for a life within the home range of their mothers. In contrast, young males move well away at around two years of age

Breeding
Breeding is continuous, with most young born January-August. Gestation is 29-30 days. Sexual maturity is reached at 14 months in females, 19 months

in males. The female has four teats in a forward opening pouch. She produces one young, which remains in the pouch for 9-10 months. Weaning takes place 12-17 months. The young wallaby is left in a hiding place amongst tussocks or long grass while the mother feeds.

Status
Abundant - this species appears to have benefited from European settlement with large numbers in forestry and agricultural areas.

SUGGESTED DIET
Per Animal – Per Day
Increase during breeding season

MACROPOD MIX:

Adult male	500 grams
Adult female	400 grams
Juveniles	300 grams

Daily
2/3 cup Carrot, 1/3 cup Maize

Twice a week
½ Sweet Potato, Apple, Greens, Fresh Lucerne

Ad Lib
Meadow Hay
Fresh branches when available (Eucalypt, Acacia, etc)

CLEAN WATER AVAILABLE AT ALL TIMES

Recommended Enclosure Size

Minimum enclosure floor area	Maximum number of animals	Minimum Height	Increased floor area for each additional animal
300 sq m	1	1.8 m	150 sq m

** Watch for signs of incompatibility as relationships can change quickly*

BLACK-TAILED WALLABY
Wallabia bicolor - Desmarest 1804

Size: Head & Body 69-76 cm; Tail 69-76 cm
Weight: Males 17kg; Females 13kg

Wallabia – 'small kangaroo'. *bicolor* - 'two coloured' refers to the contrast between its dark brown back and the rusty-yellow ventral part of its body. Also known as **Swamp Wallaby, Black Pademelon, Fern Wallaby.**

Description
An assortment of genetic, reproductive, dental and behavioural characteristics set this wallaby far apart from others. The only species in this genus, the Swamp Wallaby is a thick-set animal. It has very dark brown/black dense, flecked fur, with a rusty-orange belly, and distinctive pale check-stripes.

Habitat
Ranging from the tropical rainforests of Northern Queensland, to the cool-temperate woodlands of south-western Victoria, the Swamp Wallaby lives in thick undergrowth in forest, woodland and heath habitats.

Diet
Swamp Wallabies are generalist browsers, eating a wide range of plants, including shrubs, ferns and coarse material such as sedges and grasses.

Social Interaction
Usually a solitary animal, by day it sleeps in dense vegetation, coming out at night to feed. When hopping the Swamp Wallaby keeps its head low, has its body bent over, and holds its tail straight.

Breeding
Females reach sexual maturity at 15-18 months. Breeding is continuous, although births peak April - September. The female has four teats in a forward opening pouch. Gestation is 35-37 days. She rears a single young, which leaves the pouch at 8-9 months, but remains dependent until 15-16 months of age. Like other marsupials, the Swamp Wallaby exhibits

embryonic diapause; but differs from most marsupials in the fact that it mates 8 days before the birth of an established foetus - thus creating a gestation period longer than the oestrous cycle.

Status
Common over much of their distribution range.

SUGGESTED DIET
Per Animal – Per Day
Increase during breeding season

MACROPOD MIX:

Adult male	500 grams
Adult female	400 grams
Juveniles	300 grams

Daily
2/3 cup Carrot, 1/3 cup Maize

Twice a week
½ Sweet Potato, Apple, Greens, Fresh Lucerne

Ad Lib
Meadow Hay
Fresh branches when available (Eucalypt, Acacia, etc)

CLEAN WATER AVAILABLE AT ALL TIMES

Recommended Enclosure Size

Minimum enclosure floor area	Maximum number of animals	Minimum Height	Increased floor area for each additional animal
300 sq m	1	1.8 m	150 sq m

Watch for signs of incompatibility as relationships can change quickly

Red-necked Wallaby *Macropus rufogriseus*
Black-tailed Wallaby *Wallabia bicolor*

Red-necked Wallaby with pouch young *Macropus rufogriseus*

ANTILOPINE WALLAROO
Macropus antilopinus - Gould 1841

Size: Head & Body 80-106 cm; Tail 69-81.5 cm
Weight: Males 37-47 kg; Females 17.5-25 kg

Macropus – 'large foot' referring to the extreme length of its hindfoot.
antilopinus – 'antelope-like' referring to the supposed similarity between
the body hair of this species and that of an antelopes.
Also known as **Antilopine Kangaroo, Antelope Kangaroo.**

Description
The Antilopine Wallaroo's outward appearance and behaviour is similar to
that of the Red and Grey Kangaroo. It is a slender and long-limbed animal,
with soft fur, reddish to sandy upper parts and white underneath. Its lower
jaw is pale, with no definite cheek-stripe. The tips of the paws and hind feet
are black. Its tail is thick at the base and tapers only gradually.

Habitat
Occupying an ecological niche, the Antilopine Wallaroo inhibits the
savannah woodlands in monsonnal tropical areas of northern Australian,
where Red or Grey Kangaroos are absent.

Diet
This Wallaroo can be seen grazing on grasses in open country, on relatively
flat land at any time of the day or night, depending on the temperature.

Social Interaction
On very hot days, the Antilopine Wallaroo can be found resting among
trees, shrubbery or in rocky areas with water close by. It is gregarious by
nature, and groups consist of 3-8 members, although up to 30 individuals
have been noted, but these appear to be gatherings of smaller groups.

Breeding
Although births can occur throughout the year, breeding is usually timed so
that the young leave the pouch when grass is becoming readily available, in
the early part of the summer wet season. The female has four teats in a

forward opening pouch, but usually rears only one young. Gestation is 32-35 days. The young first leave the pouch at 7 months, permanently by 9 months, and are fully weaned at 12 months. Independence is reached by 15 months. Sexual maturity is reached in females at 24 months.

Status
In the western regions, the Antilopine Wallaroo is seen as common.

SUGGESTED DIET
Per Animal – Per Day
**Increase during breeding season*

MACROPOD MIX

Adult male	700 grams
Adult female	400 grams
Juvenile male	400 grams
Juvenile female	350 grams

Extras
½ cup Maize (daily)
1x Carrot, Sweet Potato, Apples (chopped - twice a week)

Ad Lib
Meadow Hay, Fresh Lucerne, Green Grass

Browse
Fresh branches available (Eucalypt, Acacia, Native Mint Bush etc)

CLEAN WATER AVAILABLE AT ALL TIMES

Recommended Enclosure Size

Minimum enclosure floor area	Maximum number of animals	Minimum Height	Increased floor area for each additional animal
1,000 sq m	1	2 m	500 sq m

**Watch for signs of incompatibility as relationships can change quickly.*

COMMON WALLAROO
Macropus robustus - Gould 1840

Size: Head & Body 110-198 cm; Tail 53-90 cm
Weight: Males up to 46 kg; Females up to 25 kg

Macropus – 'large foot' referring to the extreme length of the hindfoot.
robustus – 'robust' referring to the animals rather stocky build.
Also known as **Euro, Eastern Grey Wallaroo, Red Wallaroo, Roan Wallaroo, Barrow Island Wallaroo, Hill Kangaroo, Biggada.**

Description
Extending from eastern to western coasts of mainland Australia, the eastern population (on both sides of the Great Dividing Range) has shaggy grey fur, known as the Common Wallaroo. Further west to the coast of Western Australia, a shorter furred animal, reddish in colour is known as the Euro.

Habitat
This Wallaroo occurs in a wide range of habitats, from wet sclerophyll forests to arid tussock grassland, although usually associated with rocky slopes where it rests during the day in caves or on rock-shelves.

Diet
Emerging at night to graze on level land, preferring high-protein, low fibre grasses, it is an arid-adapted animal and does not necessarily need to drink.

Social Interaction
Usually found solitary, although sometimes forming small groups.

Breeding
Breeding can occur at any time of the year, but in arid areas this is dependent upon rainfall. The female is half the weight of a mature male. She has four teats in a forward opening pouch and rears one young. The gestation period of 33-35 days occurs within the oestrus cycle so that birth is quickly followed by a post-partum oestrus and mating – despite the suckling of the newborn young. The resulting embryo remains inactive until the first young is ready to leave the pouch - at around 8-9 months, but

remains dependent until 12-16 months of age. The female becomes mature in her second year (18-24 months old), males at 24 months of age.

Status

Although seen as abundant, the small Victorian population of the Eastern Wallaroo is particularly vulnerable because of its apparent isolation.

SUGGESTED DIET
Per Animal – Per Day
Increase during breeding season

MACROPOD MIX

Adult male	700 grams
Adult female	400 grams
Juvenile male	400 grams
Juvenile female	350 grams

Extras
½ cup Maize (daily)
1x Carrot, Sweet Potato, Apples (chopped - twice a week)

Ad Lib
Meadow Hay, Fresh Lucerne, Green Grass

Browse
Fresh branches available (Eucalypt, Acacia, Native Mint Bush etc)

CLEAN WATER AVAILABLE AT ALL TIMES

Recommended Enclosure Size

Minimum enclosure floor area	Maximum number of animals	Minimum Height	Increased floor area for each additional animal
1,000 sq m	1	2 m	500 sq m

Watch for signs of incompatibility as relationships can change quickly.

Kangaroo Island Kangaroo *Macropus fuliginosus fuliginosus*

Red Kangaroo female with young *Macropus rufus*

Red Kangaroo Male *Macropus rufus*

WESTERN GREY KANGAROO
Macropus fuliginosus - Desmarest 1817

Size: Head & Body 95-220 cm; Tail 43-100 cm
Weight: Males up to 53 kg; Females up to 27 kg

Macropus – 'big foot' refers the extreme elongation of the animals hindfoot.
fuliginosus – 'sooty' refering to the animals dull brown colour.
Also known as **Black-faced Kangaroo, Mallee Kangaroo.**

Description
A large kangaroo, there is much variation in the colouring of this species. In the west are more grey-brown and appear slender, while in South Australia, Victoria and New South Wales they are more solidly built, and a darker brown. The most distinctive form of the species lives on Kangaroo Island, which are a darker sooty brown, and has shorter limbs, ears and tail.

Habitat
This Kangaroo is found in a broad band across southern Australia, in areas of constant or winter-dominant rainfall. It occupies slightly drier parts than the Eastern Grey. It inhabits almost all dry forest, dry woodland, mallee scrub and wet and dry heath vegetation associated with its range.

Diet
The favoured foods of the Western Grey Kangaroo are grasses, although other foods such as forbs will be eaten. When these foods disappear during drought conditions, the Kangaroos will browse on shrubs.

Social Interaction
By day the Western Grey Kangaroo can be found sleeping in the shade. At night it grazes in groups (mobs).

Breeding
A male Western Grey reaches sexual maturity between 20-30 months of age, females at around 14-17 months. Breeding can occur throughout the year, although most births appear between October-March. This species does not appear to undergo embryonic diapause. The female has four teats

in a forward-opening pouch. Gestation is 28-33 days. A single young is born, and immediately attaches itself to a teat. It first leaves the pouch at around 10 months, but continues to suckle for a further 6 months. Independence is reached between 12-16 months of age.

Status
The Western Grey is widespread and relatively abundant appearing secure.

SUGGESTED DIET
Per Animal – Per Day
**Increase during breeding season*

MACROPOD MIX

Adult male	700 grams
Adult female	400 grams
Juvenile male	400 grams
Juvenile female	350 grams

Extras
½ cup Maize (daily)
1x Carrot, Sweet Potato, Apples (chopped - twice a week)

Ad Lib
Meadow Hay, Fresh Lucerne, Green Grass

Browse
Fresh branches available (Eucalypt, Acacia, Native Mint Bush etc)

CLEAN WATER AVAILABLE AT ALL TIMES

Recommended Enclosure Size

Minimum enclosure floor area	Maximum number of animals	Minimum Height	Increased floor area for each additional animal
1,000 sq m	1	2 m	500 sq m

**Watch for signs of incompatibility as relationships can change quickly.*

EASTERN GREY KANGAROO
Macropus giganteus - Shaw 1790

Size: Head & Body 96-230 cm; Tail 43-110 cm
Weight: Males up to 66 kg; Females up to 32 kg

Macropus – 'big foot' refers the extreme elongation of the animals hindfoot.
giganteus – 'gigantic' this species was early regarded as a relative of the
Jerboa. Looked upon as a rodent, it was indeed gigantic!
Also known as **Forester, Scrub Kangaroo, Scrubber.**

Description
It has soft brownish-grey fur on its head and body with a paler grey-white belly. It has a hairy muzzle with fine hairs between the nostrils and upper lip. It has relatively large ears, and its tail is grey-brown with a black tip.

Habitat
Inhabiting a less arid range than the Western Grey, the Eastern Grey ranges in eastern half of the continent from Cape York to Victoria and Tasmania. It can be found in dry sclerophyll forests, woodlands and open grassy plains.

Diet
Eastern Greys will graze in open areas for up to 10 hours a day. Their incisors are shaped to enable the cropping of grass close to the ground.

Social Interaction
Living in mobs comprising of related females and sub-adult males. Active in the evenings and at night, often heard making a series of clucking sounds, or if alarmed, a guttural cough. Days are spent resting in the shade and safety of trees, which prevent the animals overheating.

Breeding
Breeding occurs throughout the year, with the majority of young being born October-March. Females become sexually mature at 16-24 months, males 20-36 months. The female has four teats in a forward opening pouch. Gestation is 35-38 days. She rears a single young, which leaves the pouch at

10-11 months (she will have another young in the pouch), but is still suckled until 18 months. Individuals have been known to reach 20 years of age.

Status

A population count of Eastern Grey Kangaroos in 1981 was estimated at around 9 million animals – making it one of the most abundant macropod species on the mainland (but rare in Tasmania). Overall its status is secure.

SUGGESTED DIET
Per Animal – Per Day
Increase during breeding season

MACROPOD MIX

Adult male	700 grams
Adult female	400 grams
Juvenile male	400 grams
Juvenile female	350 grams

Extras
½ cup Maize (daily)
1x Carrot, Sweet Potato, Apples (chopped - twice a week)

Ad Lib
Meadow Hay, Fresh Lucerne, Green Grass

Browse
Fresh branches available (Eucalypt, Acacia, Native Mint Bush etc)

CLEAN WATER AVAILABLE AT ALL TIMES

Recommended Enclosure Size

Minimum enclosure floor area	Maximum number of animals	Minimum Height	Increased floor area for each additional animal
1,000 sq m	1	2 m	500 sq m

Watch for signs of incompatibility as relationships can change quickly.

RED KANGAROO
Macropus rufus - Desmarest 1822

Size: Head & Body 100-115 cm; Tail 82-88 cm
Weight: Males 66 kg; Females 26 kg

Macropus – 'big foot' refers the extreme elongation of the animals hindfoot.
rufus – 'red' referring to the colour of the male of the species.
Also known as **Marloo, Plains Kangaroo, Blue Flier (female).**

Description
Males found within the eastern range have red upper parts, whilst the females and males found in the western range tend to be a blue-grey. The belly is distinctly white. It has long ears and a grey tail. The fur of the Red Kangaroo reflects both heat and light.

Habitat
Red Kangaroos can be found throughout the arid and semi-arid inland regions of Australia. Their range includes deserts, grassland, scrubland, open woodlands, and heavily degraded woodlands.

Diet
Well adapted to arid regions, it is able to survive without water if sufficient green feed is available. It prefers to graze on grasses and herbs at night.

Social Interaction
Living alone unless circumstances force animals together (drought) Red Kangaroos move up to 50km overnight in search of green feed and water. By day they retreat to the shade in order to avoid overheating and conserve body water.

Breeding
Red Kangaroos have the capacity to breed continuously when conditions are favourable. A male reaches sexual maturity at 24-30 months, females at 15-20 months. She has four teats in a forward-opening pouch. The gestation period is 33 days, usually giving birth to a single young, which will leave the pouch at around 8 months, but continue to suckle for a further 4 months,

whilst a new young is within the pouch. Independence is reached at about 12-14 months of age. Individuals have been known to reach 20 years of age.

Status
Believed to be secure, their greatest influence is that of the weather, and its effect on food availability.

SUGGESTED DIET
Per Animal – Per Day
Increase during breeding season

MACROPOD MIX

Adult male	700 grams
Adult female	400 grams
Juvenile male	400 grams
Juvenile female	350 grams

Extras
½ cup Maize (daily)
1x Carrot, Sweet Potato, Apples (chopped - twice a week)

Ad Lib
Meadow Hay, Fresh Lucerne, Green Grass

Browse
Fresh branches available (Eucalypt, Acacia, Native Mint Bush etc)

CLEAN WATER AVAILABLE AT ALL TIMES

Recommended Enclosure Size

Minimum enclosure floor area	Maximum number of animals	Minimum Height	Increased floor area for each additional animal
1,000 sq m	1	2 m	500 sq m

Watch for signs of incompatibility as relationships can change quickly.

MACROPOD MIX
(to make 20 kilos)

Ingredients

Grain - Wheat	7.10 kg
- Barley	3.35 kg
- Corn	1.25 kg
Pollard	2.60 kg
Bran	1.60 kg
Lucerne Meal	1.60 kg
Coconut Meal	1.00 kg
Lime ($CaCo_3$)	850 grams
Wheat Germ	500 grams
Salt	100 grams
Vitamin Premix	50 grams

Mix Well – store in mouse/rat proof container

** Please Note:*

PASTURE REPLACEMENT PELLETS
& WOMBAT PELLETS
are also acceptable as feed
(quantity given may need to be adjusted to suit individual animals)

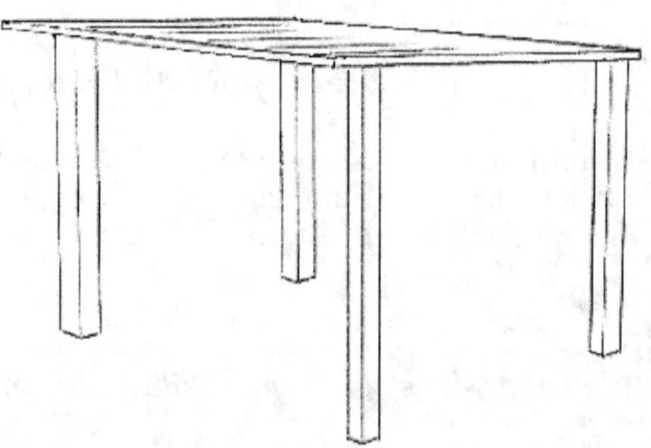

Roofed Enclosure for
Feeding Station

WALLABY MIX:

5 buckets Lucerne Chaff

1 bucket Crushed Corn

1 bucket Pasture Replacement Pellets

KANGAROO MIX:

5 buckets Lucerne Chaff

3 buckets Crushed Corn

1 bucket Pasture Replacement Pellets

Black-tailed Wallaby Joey *Wallabia bicolor*

CAPTURING, HANDLING & TRANSPORTATION

The capture and handling of all wildlife must be performed as quickly and efficiently as possible, to avoid potential injury or captive myopathy #.

All animals should be securely confined when transporting – taping cardboard boxes down, tying the end of pillowcases as well as fastening boxes within the car and leaving windows open for extra ventilation. It is not recommended carrying animals in the boot of a car as they can be affected by the toxic fumes emitted from the cars exhaust.

Smaller Macropods (Wallabies, Pademelons, etc)

In most instances, small macropods (less than 15kg) can be physically restrained. These macropods are most likely to inflict wounds via biting or scratching. They can be captured by using a hoop net, or firmly grasping the animal at the base of the tail as it hops past. An alternative method is to herd the animal into a standing net. Once in the net, the animal must be attended to immediately to minimise the period of struggling. It can then be carried a short distance by the tail base (held at arms length), or placed headfirst into a hessian sack. Once in the bag it should be suspended as animals are likely to jump about if placed on the ground. This can then be placed in a deep box filled with straw or hay for transporting.

Larger Macropods (Kangaroos, Wallaroos, etc)

Larger macropods are often highly strung and panic easily, making them more difficult to handle and may require some form of sedation. Their hind legs and forearms can inflict serious injury. Their capture usually requires the help of several handlers and a large hoop bag. One person grasps the tail base, while the others restrain its hind legs and head. It can then be sedated. Hessian wool packs or a stretcher can help in the transportation. If travelling some distance, a specially constructed well-ventilated wooden crate with a deep layer of bedding material, allowing the animal to stand on all fours and turn around is advisable. As the animal may jump, a mesh ceiling (which can be padded on the inside) to avoid damage to its head and neck is also suggested.

#Capture myopathy is a disease associated with the capture or handling of mammals and birds. Its main effects are on skeletal muscle and cardiac muscle – where the breakdown product of the damaged muscle causes kidney damage, and the production of coffee-coloured urine.

Red Kangaroo *Macropus rufus*

FOX-PROOFING OUTDOOR ENCLOSURES

"With the abundance of prey available, and little in the way of competition, foxes have found the Australian environment an ideal habitat. This species is now the most common, and the most destructive, of the introduced predators" (Green & Osborne 1994).

- Plan your enclosure to be constructed **inside out.** The enclosure should have no internal sharp projections or corners, and no loose wires.

- Perimeter fence of 2 m high, with an internal fence of 1.8 m high, and ideally the fence continued underground to stop animals digging out (30 cm is sufficient).

- Treated pine poles - 3 metre poles 100mm–125mm thick. Position poles 5 metres apart, 450mm-600mm deep into the ground, or galvanised star pickets (240 cm long).

- A single row of 1.8 metre x 35mm, or 1.8 metre Dingo weld mesh (which has gradient spacing from, 100mm x 70mm gaps) fixed to the pine poles on the *inside* of the enclosure, or a double row of 105 cm x 4cm hole size x 1.4 mm thickness wire netting.

- Line with opaque material, such as hessian, providing a visual barrier to minimise stress.

The thickness of the pole dictates the distance the hot-wire or electric fence is from the actual fencing wire. Plastic insulator clips are fixed to the pine poles on the outside, and the hot wire runs through these. Fix the insulators approximately 100mm lower than the fencing wire. The hot wire should be no more than 100mm-125mm, or the pole thickness, out from the fencing wire. The fox will have great difficulty manoeuvring under or over the electric hot wire. At the base of the fencing wire, parallel to the ground, clip 300mm x 35mm x 1.4mm mesh to the fence and pin down flat. This prevents the fox from digging under. Mow the area first, then the grass will grow through, which can be later maintained.

When leaving openings for a gate, position a pine log between the gate opening poles and level with the ground surface. Fix the netting (same as above) to the edge of the pole and pin it down. This ensures the gate opens into the enclosure, which enables the electric fence to be strung across the gate opening.

NB: Chain mesh fences are also ideal (although more expensive) use a wire arm with ceramic insulator – same distances apply.

HOUSING LARGER MACROPODS

- Enclosures should be as large as possible to reduce health and reproductive problems, and well grassed.
- Faeces should be removed daily.
- Adequate shelter, feeding stations and tree cover should be avail- able to reduce aggression and stress in animals.
- A wooden shelter can be built for these animals, or alternatively a large old galvanised water tank cut in half (check for sharp edges) can be used.
- Place shelters with opening towards north (greatest protection from cold southerly winds).
- Hay can be placed inside for animals' comfort (useful as a barrier for a sick animal to be kept within tank for recovery).
- Feeding stations should be covered, protected from the wind, and easy to clean.
- Fresh water should always be provided (self-watering is not recommended) and completely changed at least once a day.
- Any shade trees will need to be protected with tree guards.

Macropod Yard

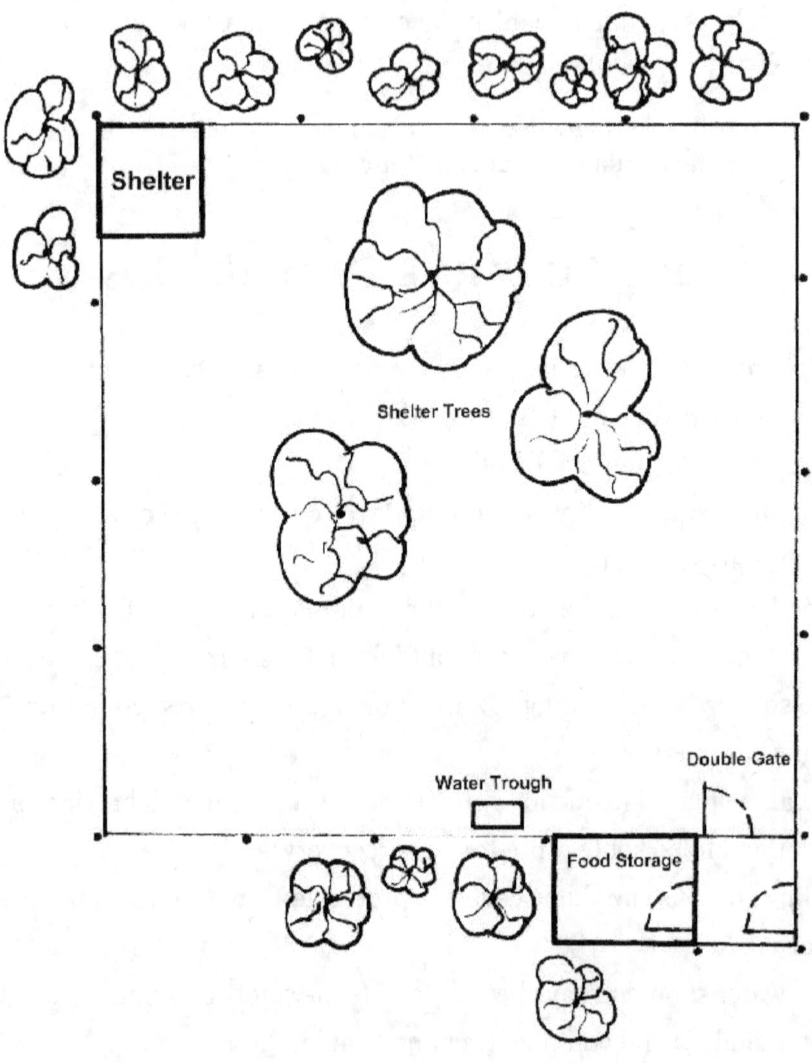

Black-tailed Wallaby *Wallabia bicolor*

Basic First Aid

Bleeding
Severe bleeding - apply pressure directly to the wound. Place a clean bandage firmly over the wound. Try and keep the animal calm, and get to a vet ASAP.

Breathing
If animal is unconscious, it should be placed in a position with the head slightly above the level of the stomach, and the head and neck extended to ensure the animal can breathe freely and to prevent choking.

Broken Bones
Bandage with a clean cloth as lightly and as straight as possible. Administer treatment to stop infection. If a compound fracture take animal to a vet ASAP.

Burns
Gradually cool the area by submerging in water or using a cold compress. Gently wrap the area with a clean, wet cloth. If severe get animal to a vet – burns can be life threatening.

Claw Infections
Commonly found at the base of the claw - immerse twice a day in a mild peroxide solution, followed by Betadine and remove all dead tissue.

Cuts
Cleanse with a spray of warm salty water. Apply a mild antiseptic. Leave and allow blood to clot - but watch closely, wounds can turn septic overnight.

Dehydration
Offer small drinks of oral rehydration solutions repeatedly for first 24 hours. If severe, a vet may be required to give intravenous fluids.

Fire Victims

Apart from the obvious burns, fire victims often suffer from respiratory trouble and pneumonia. A Multibex injection given immediately will give some relieve. Treat as for shock, and seek veterinary advice.

Heat Stress

A Mammals normal body temperature is 35-37°c.
Place the animal in a cool environment – gradually lower its body temperature using wet towels, fans, etc. Treat as for dehydration.

Hypothermia

An external temperature of 32-35°c is recommended. Gradually warm the animal with a constant, artificial heat source - inside your clothing, light bulb, electric head pad (or hot water bottle short-term only). Do not give food or water until the normal body temperature is reached.

Infections

Such as toxoplasmosis, enteritis and salmonellosis are caused through the feeding of whole animals or contaminated meats. Freezing the meat and providing only butcher-quality fresh meat will help avoid these fatal diseases.

Lumpy Jaw

Caused by necrobacillosis infection in the animals' gum. Signs are excessive salivation and chewing, and rapid swelling of the face. Damage to the teeth and skull bones from collisions with fences, the feeding of soft foods, and stress seem to be the main causes.
Avoid feeding soft foods (eg: bread) and whole grain crops (a diet of especially formulated cubes accompanied by fresh browse is recommended). Do not overcrowd animals – infected animals should be separated immediately (the disease can be passed on via contaminated water).

Mange

Sarcoptic mange is often associated with stress. It is caused by infestations of the mite *Sarcoptes scabei*. Small bald areas with associated crusty scabs are usually the first signs of this disease, but if left untreated, large areas of the animal's body become bald and covered in thick scabs.

Obesity

Usually results from over-feeding. Regular weighing of animals and altering their diet to suit is advised.

Overcrowding

Can result in the loss of tails, ears, and toes, if not death of an animal. Keep a watchful eye on animals - especially during breeding season.

Parasites

Such as mites, ticks and fleas are common. Regular checks and appropriate measures (such as the use of pyrethrin or carbaryl) is recommended.

Poisoning

Symptoms may include vomiting, convulsions, paralysis and coma.
If animal is still coherent – try vitamin C, B12 and E with dolomite powder (these de-activate the acid) - get animal to a vet ASAP. If 1080 poisoning – the antidote needs to be administered within 20 minutes of eating the bait for the animal to have any chance of survival.

Shock

Administer Flower Essences (Emergency Essence, Rescue Remedy) or Homeopathics (such as Arnica). Keep animal warm, place in quiet and dark environment. Once warm, offer high-energy fluids (Staminade or Glucodin)

Snake Bite

Snakebites affect the nervous system – pupils become enlarged, the animal will stagger, become lethargic and collapse.
An immediate injection of Vitamin C (if on hand), or crushed sodium ascorbate tablet straight down the throat, then again in an hour and daily in food for a couple of days while animal is recovering. If practical, an antidote may be sourced

Spider-bite

Unlike a snakebite, the signs are not always as noticeable.
The bitten area will be very swollen and hard. Administer Vitamin C daily until swelling has completely subsided. The most dangerous place is near the throat (where the windpipe can be affected) – injected Vitamin C every two hours is recommended.

Stress

Being constantly harassed a dominant animal, overcrowding, lack of shelter, inadequate diet, too high/low temperature, etc can all lead to high levels of stress in captive animals. This in turn can lead to weight-loss, loss of fur, or a series of infections that often end in death. Watch animals during their activity times, while also physically checking animals during rest times regularly.

Ticks

Ticks do not kill as quickly as a snake bite – signs are lethargy and coma. Firstly treat as for snake bite, then look for the tick. Remove tick by touching it with a lightened match – do not pull out as it will inject the rest of its venom. Clean area with antiseptic (such as diluted Tea Tree Oil) until redness have gone.

Worms

Leaving intestinal worms untreated can lead to health problems. The classic signs of worm infestation are weight loss, increased/decreased appetite, poor coat condition, anaemia, diarrhoea, blood or mucous in stools, pot belly or just generally unwell. Faecal pellets should be regularly checked.

Your vet can recommend a regular worming program
Or any of these can be added to the animals meals:

Finely chopped:
Raw Carrot, Coconut, Pumpkin seeds, Sesame seeds, Figs
Apple cider vinegar
(added to the drinking
water)

Macropod Shelter

Glossary

Abundant plentiful, copious
Agile active, quick, nimble
Arboreal adapted for moving and living in trees
Arid parched with heat, dry
Arthropods animals which have jointed bodies, many legs and an exoskeleton.
Carnivorous feeding on other animals, flesh-eating
Carrion dead and putrefying flesh
Communal for common use, shared
Conical cone-shaped
Dasyurid a member of the marsupial family
Diurnal active by day
Dorsal of/on back
Drey nest of an arboreal animal (eg: ringtail possum)
Dusk twilight
Endangered Species that have very low population numbers and are in immediate danger of extinction if casual factors persist.
Endemic restricted to a particular locality
Eucalypt Australian gum tree
Extinct Species which can not be found in areas that they once inhabited, nor recorded in other likely habitats, within the past 50 years.
Fauna animals of a given region
Feral animal reverted to a wild state
Forage search for food
Gestation period in the womb between conception and birth
Gregarious sociable, living in company
Habitat area providing physical and biological conditions required by a species.
Herbivore feeds on plants
Inhabiting occupies
Insectivorous feeds on insects and other arthropods
Invertebrate animal having no spine
Joey young kangaroo or possum
Juvenile young animal
Lactation suckling, secretion of milk

Litter young produced at birth
Mammal animal that suckles its young
Marsupial live-bearing mammals (kangaroos, wombats, possums, etc) found chiefly in the Australian region where the female has a pouch (of sorts) and the young are born in a very undeveloped state
Monogamous staying with one partner
Mortality state of being
Native from a particular place
Nectarivorous feeds on nectar (as well as pollen)
Nocturnal active at night
Oestrous state of sexual receptivity in a female
Omnivorous eating all foods
Opportunistic eats a wide variety of foods – depending upon their availability and/or a pattern of breeding that is linked with irregular favourable conditions
Perennial lasting throughout the year
Placental live-bearing mammals which the embryo develops entirely in the uterus
Pouch a structure or fold of skin used for enclosing young or eggs (for Monotremes) which contains mammary glands and serves as a place for safekeeping of the developing young
Prehensile capable of grasping
Rare Species, which have small populations (usually within restricted geographical limits or localised habitats), or are widely scattered, that may become endangered or vulnerable in the future.
Remnant fragment of land remaining
Rodent gnawing animal
Scrotum pouch containing testicles
Solitary alone, single
Terrestrial living on the ground
Territorial defending home ground
Torpor dormant state
Vertebrate animal having a backbone
Vulnerable Species, which are under, threat because of decreasing numbers; Or which have been seriously depleted in the past and have not recovered.

PHOTOGRAPHES

DIAGRAMS

INDEX

BIBLIOGRAPHY & RECOMMENDED READING

Dawson, Terence J. (1995). Kangaroos: Biology of the Largest Marsupials. University of New South Wales Press.

Green, Ken., Osborne, William. (1994). Wildlife of the Australian Snow-country: A comprehensive guide to alpine fauna. Reed, Chatswood NSW.

Hand, Suzanne J. (ed.) (1995). Care and Handling of Australian Native Animals: Emergency Care and Captive Management. Royal Zoological Society of NSW/Surrey Beatty & Sons.

Menkhorst, Peter W. (ed.) (1995). Mammals of Victoria: Distribution, Ecology and Conservation. Oxford University Press, Australia.

Paltridge, Rachel & McAlpin, Steve (2002). A Guide to Rare & Threatened Animals in Central Australia. WWF Australia Publications.

Strahan, Ronald (ed.) (1981). A Dictionary of Australian Mammal Names. Australian Museum/Reed New Holland.

Strahan, Ronald (ed.) (1988). Complete Book of Australian Mammals: The National Photographic Index of Australian Wildlife. The Australian Museum/Angus & Robertson.

Strahan, Ronald (ed.) (2000). The Mammals of Australia. Revised Edition. Australian Museum/Reed New Holland.

Walraven, Erna. (1999). Care of Australian Wildlife. New Holland, Australia. Watts, Dave. (1993). Tasmanian Mammals: A Field Guide. Revised Edition. Peregrine Press, Tasmania.

White, Sharon. (1997). Caring for Australian Wildlife: a practical guide to the management of sick, injured and orphaned native animals. Australian Geographic.

Williams, Anne & Ray. (1999). Caring for Kangaroos and Wallabies. Kangaroo Press, an imprint of Simon & Schuster, East Roseville, NSW.

Also available from author:

- Kangaroo Island - a wildlife haven
- Arboreal Marsupials - caring for Possums and Gliders
- Macropods - caring from Kangaroos and Wallabies
- Carnivorous Marsupials - caring for Dunnarts, Quolls and more
- Creating a frog-friendly backyard
- Fattus Wombatus - a children's story
- Tasty Treats for your Best Friend
- Keeping Backyard Chickens
- Discovering the Bears & Wolves of Hudson Bay, Canada
- Wild About Borneo - in search of the Organ-Utan
- Sri Lanka, Pearl of the Indian Ocean
- A Taste of Vietnam - a photographic essay
- Turning Japanese - a photographic essay

Long-nosed Potoroo *Potorous tridactylus*

9 798376 889701